ASHES
IN PARADISE

Ashes in Paradise

Jeff Friedman

MadHat Press
Cheshire, Massachusetts

MadHat Press
MadHat Incorporated
PO Box 422, Cheshire, MA 01225

The Library of Congress has assigned
this edition a Control Number of
2023948293

ISBN 978-1-952335-69-3 (paperback)

Words by Jeff Friedman
Cover image and design by Marc Vincenz

www.MadHat-Press.com

First Printing
Printed in the United States of America

Always for Colleen

Table of Contents

Section 3

Section 4

And after a while the world moves on. The ocean swallows and regurgitates, valleys send off steam and the horses pass from the black field into the white field. There is also heard the resounding clash of air on air.

—Zbigniew Herbert

Hole in My Head

There's a hole in my head the size of a half dollar—and who knows how deep? The surgeon advised me to leave the wound open, because, she said, it would heal faster, but it's already been two years. When I go out, birds plunge at my bright dome. I swing my arms to keep them away, but some still land and dip their beaks into the hole as if searching for insects or worms. Something must scare them because they take off quickly. I clean out the hole with a damp piece of cloth and find leaves, stray hairs, pebbles, coins, blessings and aphorisms. For a while I wore a large bandage over the hole, but then my head would swell as if it were filling up with fluid. When I'd slowly remove the bandage, thoughts shot out and showered through the air like glitter. Always, a few broken thoughts would be stuck to the bandage. Each day, I stare into the mirror and hold a mirror over my head to get a good look inside the hole. I see some creature deep below, turning over to show its orange belly, and numerous clichés bobbing near the surface. When I shift the mirror, my head disappears, and only the hole remains.

Section 1

The Touch

Everything Midas touched turned to gold, but everything I touch, except myself, disappears. He wished for his own curse, for gold over everything else, but I simply wanted to touch others and feel their skin, their bones, their pulse. I wanted to breathe them in, to know them inside me, but each person I touched vanished before I could feel anything. And each thing I touched—each dish, each chair, each counter—disappeared also as if it never existed. Where there was a couch, there is only the memory of a couch. Where there was a lamp, there is only darkness. I am surrounded by holes. And all my people are gone, memories also. Touching others once brought me pleasure, but now I touch no one, and no one disappears.

Catching the Monster

On Main Street, I spot the monster in the crowd. He's clean-shaven, but there are red nicks on his cheeks and chin. He's got long claws that can rip a chest apart in seconds. No one in the crowd appears to notice that the monster is among them. I follow closely weaving in and out until I'm almost stepping on his heels. Suddenly he turns to face me. "You're a monster," I say. He licks the stain of blood from his lips. "Is that so bad?" he asks. "There are many missing," I answer, "and bones scattered throughout the city." Without even a glance, people walk by or around us. Neon signs blink. Cars jam the noisy streets growing jumpy, music blasting from open windows. "There are always many missing, always trails of clues leading everywhere and nowhere," he says. I grip his forearm, causing him to grimace. "I'm taking you in." The monster breathes in my face. His breath is sweet, as if he has eaten a sweet meat. He stares deep into my eyes, searching for my secrets. "If you believe in monsters, perhaps you are a monster," he says. "Isn't that what all monsters say?" I ask. "Point well taken," he answers, "but you do have a powerful jaw, yellow eyes and spotted skin—like the rest of us monsters." I cuff his wrist to mine, head to the station to turn us both in—for the reward.

Spring in the Air

In checkout lane three at the grocery, I feel my nose twitch inside my mask. The two carts closest to the cashier are six feet apart, but the rest of us are much closer together. While some shoppers chat briefly, laughing at jokes, while some lean over their carts for support, and some pull out hand sanitizer, rubbing their hands briskly, I scrunch my face to hold back a sneeze. When the guy in the next lane asks me a question, I begin to answer and without warning, the sneeze escapes. I'm shaken, but quickly hold up my hands and shout into my mask, "Allergies—I'm not sick," but the other shoppers look at me as if I'm dangerous. Before I can do anything about it, I sneeze again, and my mask sails off like a large butterfly, floating over heads until it lands on a grocery conveyor belt two lanes away, touching an avocado. The cashier removes the mask with her gloved hand…. The shopper says "no" to the avocado, which the cashier places near her register. The other shoppers move as far away from me as they can. I try to reassure them, but a third even more powerful sneeze explodes from my mouth and nose. The automatic doors open. The plexiglass windows shake. The shoppers hit the floor, holding their breath, their heads buried in their hands. A sea of droplets and aerosols hangs over them. There's no way for me to clear the air now. For a long moment the store is silent. The only other person standing is the cashier in lane five. She smiles and signals me to come ahead. "But I'm not next in line," I say. "You go!" the other shoppers shout from the floor, so I wheel around them, pay for my groceries quickly, and leave the store without another sneeze.

About Face

When my lover removes her mask, I see her face for the first time. "You're beautiful," I say and touch her cheek as she lies next to me.

"You said I was beautiful before. Were you lying?"

"I was talking about your mask," I answer. "Now I'm talking about your face."

She unstraps my mask and removes it gently. "Nice," she says, but looks surprised.

"Something wrong?" I ask.

"No, it's just you look so different."

"Different good or bad?"

"Your face is more like a kitty than a leopard, more of a cloud than a sky, more shadow than sun."

"What does that mean?" I ask.

"Without your mask, you're a little displaced, out of sorts, a metaphor adrift, a subject searching for a predicate."

"You're my predicate."

Too close together, we're breathing each other's droplets and aerosols, inhaling and exhaling them. "It's not safe," I say, "We should put the masks back on."

"Wouldn't we already be sick after all this time?" she asks

"How would we know? There might not be symptoms for days—for years."

She tosses her mask on the nightstand. "I'm fine without it," she says.

I reach over her to retrieve hers, but she stops me, and then straps the band of my mask over my ears and positions it on my face. "That's better," she says and closes her eyes. I turn over but remain restless all night. Before too long, she is sleeping, her face sweet and calm, her breath like soft kisses on my neck.

The Boy with Holes

The officers who shot the boy repeatedly watched him fall face first, his arms and legs jerking until all movement ceased. They kept their distance, holstering their weapons, sure that it was all over, but the boy rose, his sweet face dirt stained. He walked slowly toward the officers. Light poked through the holes in his body. The ground was wet with blood. They stepped back and took out their weapons again. "I've never seen anything like this before," one officer said. The other agreed. Though they told him to stop and get down on his knees, the boy kept walking until he stood so close he touched one officer on the arm. Like a breath grazing the skin, his hand felt weightless. The officer cocked his gun and held it to the boy's head. Crows gathered around them. The trees rustled. The red sun flared so intensely they had to squint to see his shape, and then the boy vanished. Now all they could see were the holes.

Bad Day for the Shooters

They shoot holes in the river, but the holes close up, and the river runs on. They shoot the shadows that leap out of the river, and the shadows fall, bleeding light. They shoot the ducks from the branches, but they aren't ducks. "What did we shoot?" one asks. "I don't know," another answers, "but they needed shooting." The shoot the bellies off clouds, but the clouds grow new bellies, so they shoot them again. They shoot the lizards lounging on rocks, but the lizards don't budge. In town, they shoot the windows on Main Street and the beggars on the sidewalks, and then there are more windows, more beggars cupping their palms. They check their guns, reload. They shoot the mothers pushing their babies in strollers, but the mothers keep pushing their strollers, and the babies laugh like dolls with computer chips. They shoot grandmothers and grandfathers who rise like vapor and rain down on them until they run for shelter, their hats flying off, their guns dripping puddles.

No One Visits

No one came to our home, uninvited. He knocked on the door so many times and so loudly we had to answer. "Who's there?"

"No one," he said. "Who are you?"

We opened the door partway. "We live here. What do you want?"

"To be your friend," he said as he pushed past us.

"We have enough friends," we said, but no one ignored our comment.

He sat at the table and ate the pears and grapes. Next, he cut the cake and ate a large chunk, even though we objected. We cleaned the crumbs from the counter and the table. We cleared away his plate.

"What's for dinner," he asked.

"Nothing," we answered. "We weren't expecting company."

No one opened the Fridge and found the cooked chicken and sweet potatoes. He ate his dinner cold, while we shot each other glances blaming each other for letting him in. We hinted that it was time to leave, but he ignored the hints. Then we each grabbed one of his arms to lead him to the door, but he was too strong and led us into the living room, where he took off his shoes and sat on the couch.

"Let me tell you a story," he said, so we sat across from him, hoping if we listened to his story, he might go away. But no one told us a story that digressed for hours.

"Does this story have a point or even an ending?" we asked.

"My story is your story." He yawned as if he were tired of telling the story, and then we yawned also, stretching our arms, our eyelids growing heavy.

But no one only pretended to be sleepy. He put us to sleep in our chairs, drawing the covers over us. No one watched our eyes flutter and then entered our dreams. Now no one lives inside us.

Arrest

Early morning on Pleasant Street, a burly cop in plainclothes flashed his badge in my face. "Malik Jones, you're under arrest." "I'm not Malik Jones," I answered and attempted to walk around him, but he blocked my path. A woman dressed in a work outfit speeded up as she walked past. I took out my wallet to show him who I am, but he grabbed it from me, riffling through it. "You have nine different drivers licenses, all with different names," he said. "And your photo is on each of them." "Ten," I answered, "but not one of them has the name Malik Jones." The sun shone in his face. He was a pleasant-looking man with blue eyes and husky eyebrows. He didn't have a gun, and his jacket and pants were rather scruffy. "What did Malik do? I asked. "Plenty," he said. "You should know." The sidewalk was becoming crowded with people. Many glanced at us, but not one of them stopped to see if something was wrong. Shops lit up on both sides of the street. Pigeons poked around for food under the high curbs. He clamped my forearm with a vicious grip and led me to the station. Inside the door, several cops sprang forward. Separating the burly man and me, they cuffed him for impersonating an officer. "Could have fooled me," I said. "We're sorry this happened" When I headed for the door, they stopped me, and one officer took out his gun. "What did I do?" "Nothing," they said, "but you have 10 identities." "Since when is that a crime?" I asked. They looked at one another and then back at me, puzzled. "You've got a point," the officer with the gun said. "However, an arrest is an arrest." They locked me up and then sent out their best men to catch Malik.

What's Left

When you're sleeping, you're not a racist, except your dreams are racist—only one color. When you awake, it's clear to you that there are racists in your cupboards, your refrigerator, your couch and chairs, even in your bedroom—in the blankets and sheets. You beat the sheets and blankets, and racists rise in the dust boasting of their crimes. Next you vacuum the air and empty the bag. You stuff the blankets and sheets in the hot-water wash and the dryer at the hottest setting. No racists can survive that, you think. You dump the contents of the cupboards and refrigerator in the trash. You scrub the counters and the floors until they shine and are racist-free. Then you head to the bathroom with your cleaning pail and solvents, and the racists plead for mercy, but you disinfect the tub, the basin and toilet until there is only silence. You look into the mirror and smile, proud of yourself for all that you've accomplished, for wreaking havoc on racists, and then you get a glimpse of a dark smoke in your eyes. What's inside? you wonder. You peel your skin and inside you find another racist. "I'm not a bad racist. I don't believe in lynching. And I've never refused to serve anyone," the racist says. "You can live with me." But you don't believe it, so you ram your skeleton into the wall until the bones fall to the floor. You collect your flesh and bones and throw them into the woodstove. You light the kindling and watch the smoke being drawn up the chimney, then you close the doors and listen to the flames as the room grows warm in your emptiness.

Truth

With torches, they set truth on fire and laugh as it howls in pain. They smear their faces with the ashes and run through the streets. "Truth is dead," they shout, "Truth is dead." Some of them set fire to shops and houses. Some hurtle through windows, their flames flashing in the shattered glass. Others slough off their skins and hover over the streets like dead gods. Others climb to the tops of buildings and leap as if they believed their own myths. Others nail themselves to trees. A strong wind rips through town. Small birds plunge through the smoke. The ashes swirl, then drift for days until they dissolve in the rays of the sun or settle on the tongues of children.

The Beggar

The river swallowed the beggar. On bright days, we could see him suspended not far below the surface, holding out his cup, his lips moving. Bubbles rose to the surface, but no sound. We pitched coins into the water, watching them bob up and down until they slowly sank. None went into the cup. Some of us laid bills down to see what he would do. Turning dark, the bills drifted above him. He reached up, but they were beyond his grasp. We built a fire and chanted for him to come out of the water. Still he remained where he was. The fire died down, and the wood turned to ash. We left a stack of bills where he could see it, positioned a rock to hold the bills in place, and hid in the trees, placing bets on how long it would take him to pocket the money. After hours, he hadn't risen. The rock was still there, but the money had disappeared. We stared down into the water to see if he had it; but his cup was empty, his arm still reaching toward us as if waving. "Just like him," we said, "to hide the money we've given him and pretend he has nothing." Small fish swam into his mouth and buried themselves in his pockets.

Night in the Prison

At night, the prisoners clang their tin cups against the cell bars. At first, we remain in our chairs and ignore the clanging, but it becomes so intolerable we enter the cellblock and take away their tin cups and give them paper cups. Though we think we have solved the problem, soon the clanging starts up again, so we enter the cellblock and remove everything that might be used to clang against the bars. Before we can even lock the door, it continues. Now we remove the bars. "What kind of prison is this?" the prisoners ask, "with no metal cups or bars." "No more commotion," we say. "Back to your cells." Then we shut the lights and sit in our chairs outside the cell block. Satisfied, we nod at each other. For a long time, there is silence. Just as our eyes close and our chins sink, the metallic percussion jolts us. We enter again, but this time, we remove the prisoners and ourselves, exiting the prison in a single line, the echoes of tin cups clanging in the dark behind us.

Light at the End of the Tunnel

You say, "There's a light at the end of the tunnel," but what if there is no end? We've been in it for days, weeks, months. Perhaps even a year has passed since we entered. "There was a light that led us into the tunnel," I answer. "How do you know that the light at the end of the tunnel won't lead us someplace worse." We're on foot, having run out of gas a long time ago— our car abandoned like so many others. We still walk at a brisk pace, but we both have begun to tire. "Shh," you say. "Listen." I listen for footsteps and the sound of breath. There are others in the tunnel, but we avoid each other as much as we can in the dark, though occasionally we bump into someone or someone bumps into us. No one stops to talk. We all just keep going. When you lead, I put my hand on your shoulder, and when I lead, you do the same. This way, we've stayed together. I imagine the sun on our faces, and birds flying into the trees. I imagine lying in the soft grass and sleeping with you next to me. "If we keep walking, we'll come to the end of the tunnel," you say, but now I can't even remember entering a tunnel. For all I know, we're walking under collapsed stars and the darkest moon in the universe.

Our Puppets

At dusk, our puppets leave their cages and go out hunting. They swoop down on small rodents, gashing their bellies as they dart through the grass. They leap on squirrels on tree branches, biting their necks. They bash into sparrows and wrens in flight, pouncing on them when they fall to the ground. They rip into cats slinking through backyards and scatter their shredded guts. They maul crows that don't leap into flight quickly enough. And they plunge into men and women who dawdle outside their houses. At dawn, our puppets come back with cat bones, feathers, tufts of black hair and nests as gifts. Their shadows act out their kills on the bright walls. Our puppets return to their cages to sleep. We lock them in, watching over their loud, violent dreams.

The Last Truth

One truth was shot while it sat in a café, sipping an Americano and writing its memoir. Another truth rose up on a stage and protested the swarm of lies that had descended on the town, clinging to heads and faces or flying down throats. The mob rushed the stage, pummeling this truth until it fell beneath them. They kicked and stomped it to death. Another truth was tortured until it confessed that it was a lie and then the spirit left its body, and only emptiness resided inside it. Many truths were burned in the public square as they screamed, "I'm telling the truth." We collected their ashes and bone in an urn and tried to bring them back to life with spells and chants, but our words had lost their belief in the power to summon. And the last truth, hiding for months in abandoned buildings, escaped into the forest. When it returned years later, no one recognized it or believed what it was saying.

Section 2

My Enemy

"Get the fire extinguisher," my enemy said. "Your house is in flames." But I didn't believe him, though the flames rose around us. "The fire isn't real," I said, though the blaze was getting hotter, and smoke filled the air. "Why would I lie?" he answered. "Because you're my enemy," I said. He brushed past me and retrieved the fire extinguisher, aiming it at the fire, but nothing happened. "It's too old, I guess, or faulty, or someone else used it," I said. Now we could barely see each other, and he began coughing. "You did this," I said. "No." He threw his body at mine just as the windows exploded, and the fixtures splintered. "Stay on the ground," he said and follow me." We crawled out of the house, and then from a distance, watched it burn. Soon the trucks arrived, but it was too late. My enemy looked at me with pity in his face. "You've lost everything," he said. "No," I answered. "I still have you."

Offering

Cain could have sacrificed a goat or some sheep, but the sheep bleated plaintively, and he loved the goats' horns, the way they curled under. He mounded the fruits of the soil over sticks. He lit the fire. A delicious smoke from the charred wheat, figs, and olives rose into the sky.

The animals drooled. "Save some for us," they demanded, and he left the rest for them.

But God rejected Cain's offering. "No meat," he said.

And Abel laughed. "Don't be such a fool," he said to Cain. "Next time, give him what he wants." Abel killed three goats and burned them in a pit until they were ash and bone.

And God smiled on him while Cain bowed his head in shame and knew he would never be loved equally.

The dirt warned him about envy, though he didn't know the meaning of the word. The rock told him not to act in anger, though anger controlled him. He picked up the rock and smashed his brother's head, and his brother fell. The blood trickling out became a river.

God found Cain in the garden and banished him, marking him so he wouldn't be murdered and forbidding the fields to yield their bounty to him. When Cain picked up a rock, it was warm to his touch.

The Voice in the Bush

A fire burned in the bush outside my home. I stomped on it, but it wouldn't go out. I threw handfuls of dust on it, yet still it blazed on—though without heat. Out of the fire, a voice boomed, "Moses, Moses—" I interrupted, "I'm not Moses." "You are now," the voice stated. "Why the name change?" "You have been chosen," the voice said. I looked deep into the flame to see if I could spot a shape or a mouth, but the voice was entirely disembodied—too loud to be a trick of my imagination. "Moses, you will lead our people—" I interrupted again. "What people are you talking about?" I asked. "My people," the voice said. Not very specific, I thought. Still a voice in a flaming bush had to be considered some kind of miracle. "Where am I leading your people?" I asked. "Out of Egypt," the voice answered. "Check your GPS," I said. "This is St. Louis. Egypt's half the globe away. Nobody in St. Louis would follow me anywhere, let alone out of Egypt." Now the fire flared to a monstrous size, rising above me into a pillar. "You will crush our enemies or I will crush you," the voice commanded. "These are my neighbors," I said. "I don't get along with most of them, but I wouldn't want to crush them." "It's them or you," the voice said. The flame turned red and then slowly eased until it was only the size of a campfire. I walked away from it to the end of the driveway. Up and down the block, my neighbors were staring into their own burning bushes, their voices growing angrier like a swarm of hornets. Then they began charging at one another with raised shovels. I rolled out my garden hose and turned it full blast on my burning bush. Within seconds, the voice in the bush was only a sputter.

The Ark

"Sorry, we can't take you," Noah says. "We've got only so much room, and you're not on the list." He shoves me aside to allow two pigs to clamber up the plank, oinking to each other, their curled tails like question marks. Two giraffes follow, lowering their long necks to enter. The people and the animals create a din of continuous noise. Two mice graze my foot scurrying into the ark. I start up the plank, but Noah blocks me again. "Certainly, you can squeeze in one more," I say. "Maybe, but not you," he replies. He's too big and strong to overpower, and even if I could get past him, his wife and sons guard the entrance with their clubs. "We're saving humanity," Noah says frankly. "And you'd only be extra baggage." "I hear you need monkeys. I can be a monkey," I answer, lowering my arms to the ground and making monkey noises until a female monkey steps out, laughing. "You're the worst monkey I've ever seen," she yells. "And a poor excuse for a human," Noah adds, self righteous as always. He waves goodbye, "Wait for the next ark," and closes the hatch. The ark bobs in the river. A few drops of rain fall. I take shelter inside the hollow of a tree, but after several hours, the sun is still shining, so I step out and say a prayer for the future. God answers from a fluffy white cloud. "No storm in sight for a thousand years. The joke's on them."

Flood

As I slosh into the bathroom, the water comes up over my jean cuffs. "Honey," I shout at my lover, "Did you leave the bathtub running?" However, the handle is shut tight, and the spigot is dry. My lover splashes into the room. "I checked the faucets upstairs and downstairs. It's not coming from there either. And I shut off the main water valve." "Good work," I say. The water has now come up to our knees. We peruse the ceiling to see if the roof is the source, but it's not. "It must be coming in from below, ground water," I conclude. My lover nods. "Good to know, but how do we stop it?" "Good question: We shouldn't have let it happen in the first place." She scowls at me and then opens the door to let the water out; instead it pours in. The water breaks the windows and doors and sweeps us out of the house. The house rips from its foundations. We're rising toward the tops of the trees while houses all over the neighborhood bump against each other headed for the town. Soon the whole world is water, and we're underwater but still breathing. My lover says something, but her words come out bubbles. I say something, and bubbles flow from my mouth also. The sun shines through the flood, creating lanes of light in which we can see thousands of tiny dead creatures. Embracing each other, we rise toward the surface, but there is no surface only more water and sun. Exhausted, we spot a chain of islands in the water and swim toward them as fast as we can, but each island dissolves just as we touch it.

Dead Animal

"Let's split it," the fox said. He sat near the dead animal, watching me closely. I crouched down. "Why should I split anything with you? I'm bigger and stronger." The fox blinked. His lush tail curled in the dirt and weeds. "You have a point," he said. "But I found it, and there is enough for both of us." The crows descended around us. Then came the squirrels running up and down the tree branches. The deer vaulted through the clearing. As we faced each other, the smell of bear grew strong. "Better to share," the fox said, "than to wind up with nothing." Though I had a physical advantage, I didn't want to fight the fox for the dead animal, if I could avoid it. In the sky, hawks crossed in flight, screeching until other hawks arrived. Then came the army of ants. "Start a fire," the fox shouted. Several crawled on my leg, biting me. I struck a match and lit the weeds. The flames rose up in front of us. Some of the ants burned up in the flames, but the rest plowed through it. The hawks screeched loudly. Coyotes and bears emerged from the woods, but the blaze spread to the carcass, and before we could do anything about it, the dead animal flesh turned to ash. "It's all yours," the fox said and trotted off. The hawks and crows flew away. The bears and coyotes vanished. The squirrels ran up and down in the trees. While I backed away slowly, the ants swarmed the bones of the dead animal.

Ram in the Thicket

While the ram hid in the thicket, Abraham built an altar and mounded on it the bundle of sticks and twigs gathered by his son. He bound Isaac and laid him on the kindling. Afraid to move or make a sound, the ram kept low, out of sight, he thought. Abraham said a prayer and lifted his knife. The ram may not have understood the prayer, but he knew the meaning of the drawn knife, the blade blinking in the light. For a moment, nothing moved, not the ram, not the father's arm and not the son, who stared at the knife as if it were some foreign god. Then Abraham's face tightened as he willed himself to strike, but the muscles in his arm clenched and wouldn't move. He raised his head to the sky and appeared to be talking to someone, though no one else was there—no angel, no godly being, only particles of dust. Then Abraham nodded as though obeying an order and slowly lowered the knife to his side, loosening his grip. Rising from the altar, Isaac's body trembled. He offered his own prayer to the sun and the dust, thankful he had not become the burnt offering, thankful that God had saved him from his own father. Still he knew there would be a sacrifice. And the ram let out a sigh and was revealed, and the shrub where he was hiding shook a little as though touched by the wind.

29

The Ashes

We poured the ashes into the garden and said a prayer, a single bee flying from the roses. When we returned a day later, the flowers and plants had died, so we scooped the ashes into a container and walked down to the river where we kneeled and emptied them slowly, but instead of drifting away, they floated back to us. Again, we gathered them, but this time we spread them carefully at the base of an oak, where they lay in the shade. "This is good," we said, nodding. As the sun shone in our faces, the leaves began to wilt and fall. The birds flew out, calling angrily for us to take back our ashes. "You can't leave them here," they said. "This is our tree." So we gathered them again and took them to an open space in the cemetery. With our hands, we dug a small hole and buried the ashes, tamping down the grass and dirt. We placed a stone over the grave. As we began to walk away, we thought we heard a voice. When we turned, the stone was gone, and the grass over the small grave had turned brown. Once more, we gathered the ashes. At home, we built a fire in the fireplace and tossed them in. The bits of bone turned bright white for a moment before the fire went out.

Out of Paradise

He conjured dust to fling into the faces of enemies and friends. He conjured the mist in which death lives. He conjured fire to scorch cities and fields, and the blaze rose into a mountain. He conjured oceans to strangle the flames, and millions of arks bobbing like buoys. He conjured driftwood and shards, rocks with animal shapes pressed into them, sea creatures whose bellies were filled with treasure, birds with covenants written on their wings. Vultures hovered. Wild dogs tore at the remains. He conjured a new world in which justice reigned, and his word was eternal, but only his crimes survived.

Terrorists

We found them in cafes, sipping Americanos at tables near windows, ready to detonate bombs with their smart watches. We found them wheeling carts through the supermarket, testing the avocados for ripeness, bagging up chickpeas and figs. We found them in windows disguised as mannikins, sharply tailored, their faces perfectly calm. We found them in our neighborhoods, burying their weapons in flower gardens and laying down bags of mulch. We found them in the faces of the clouds, in the dust falling over us. We found pieces of their stars and the shards of the exploding moon. We found their swirling gases, their sloughed skins, their muted masks.

They entered our homes, vibrating in our networks, blurring our screens. Day and night, we heard them humming our songs, chanting our names, talking with our voices.

Brotherly Love

My older brother chokes me until I'm barely breathing. Then he hits me repeatedly with a rock. I laugh at him, "Go ahead—kill me." He pulls out his knife and stabs me ten times, blood pouring out of my wounds. "You're a loser," I shout, "but still my brother, and I love you." With a handgun, he shoots me six times and reloads, but instead of emptying his rounds, he kicks me in the gut. Though I'm dead, he's still not finished. He drives his car over my body many times. Triumphant, he stands over me. "What do you have to say about brotherly love now?" he asks. I get up, and we repeat the whole ceremony again, only this time, he burns my body and scatters the ashes. I float in the air above him, cling to his shoulders, stick to his hands. I am the mark on his forehead, the clouds in his eyes. Each time he tells the story of how he murdered me, I rise from his throat.

Bombs

Months ago, the bombs arrived in formation, hovering like blimps. At first, we thought they were participating in a military exercise, that they would be leaving soon, but they remained in place, silent except for a barely audible buzzing that disrupted our cellphone signals and our cable reception. "You're blocking our sun," we shouted at the bombs. "Our gardens are dying," but there was no response. We threw rocks at the bombs to get them to move, but the rocks bounced off them. We launched balloons with messages on them to no avail. We held up signs in protest and shot video footage to send to public TV. Nothing worked. The hard rain ricocheted off their surfaces. The wind didn't faze them. And snow that landed on the bombs melted. The bombs cast their shadows over us. Our town fell into despair, shops closing early and some not opening again, buildings boarded up. Stoplights went dead, and we stopped driving our cars, because of all the crashes. Still, there were some who liked the bombs and thought they protected us from enemy attacks, while others built new businesses for a new age of living with bombs. Undiscouraged, geese flew over the bombs, and hawks used them as vantage points to spot their prey.

Vacancies in the Cabinet

The King executed one minister for the suspicious odor that oozed from his skin. He executed another minister for shedding white feathers throughout the palace. He executed a mouse for pretending to be a minister, and another minister for eating all the cheese in the traps. One minister killed himself before the king could execute him, but the king had his guards lift up the dead minister and executed him anyway. He executed the minister of executions for limiting his quota of executions. He executed another minister for starting fires throughout his kingdom and another minister for putting them out. He executed the minister of crowd dispersal because of the clouds gathering around the palace. He executed the minister of his household for her devotion to the river. He executed the minister of dust over and over until he became dust, drifting down from the high windows. He executed the minister of air because too many of his subjects were still breathing. Now he summoned his ministers to the briefing, but only the minister of hair sat at the long table. "How about a shampoo and cut?" the minister asked. The king executed him too.

Section 3

Dream in the Garden

Satan came to him in his dream. He handed him a large shiny apple. "Take a bite, and you'll know everything." "I'm not Adam," he answered. "You've got the wrong dream." He threw the apple into the next garden, but as soon as it left his hand another apple appeared, just as red and shiny. "We're in a garden," Satan said. "There's the tree of knowledge, and there's a woman with lovely breasts following you, calling you Adam. I think I have the right dream." "I'm not the only guy," he replied, "with a naked woman with lovely breasts in his dreams. And we're not in a garden. We're in a dream of a garden." "This is my dream," Satan said. Now the woman held the apple, and she was hungry. Though the man ordered her to drop the apple, she ate it vigorously and tossed the core into a bush. "Delicious," she said, "I'll have another."

The Singer Who Lost Her Voice

The singer lost her voice, and though her lips were perfectly shaped around syllables, only breath came out. For seven days she remained silent, gargling salt water to soothe her throat muscles. When she attempted to sing again, her voice wouldn't sound; no matter how much effort she exerted, she couldn't coax or force it out, so she made an appointment with a specialist, who nodded knowingly, winked at her, and told her not to worry, that her voice would come back when she didn't expect it. After a long period of time, she didn't expect to hear her own voice anymore, so she thought that as the doctor predicted, it might return. Yet it didn't. Then she went to a healer, who poured warm oil down her throat. The oil soothed her throat; there was more silence. She found a witch online, who said it was a curse. The witch created a spell to remove the curse that had stolen her voice. "I can see your voice in the air flying toward you. Can you see it?" The singer shook her head. "Open your mouth and let it in." Something might have flown in her mouth; she didn't know. She closed her eyes and sang; her song was soundless. The palm reader traced the deep grooves of her palm and said, "You will sing again, but first you must live like a bird." What did that mean? Build a nest and live in a tree? Eat only seeds and nuts? learn to fly? She moved her arms as though they were wings. She ate her food in small quick bites. She puffed out her chest, threw back her head to sing, but couldn't even produce a whisper. Then she found a guru who had the answer. The guru prayed and chanted. He burned incense. "Go home," he said. "Drink this tea every night and chant these words, and you will sing." Night after night, she drank her tea and chanted the prayer silently. Then one night, she stood in the mirror, a glint in her eyes. Her voice would return now—she was sure of it. She began to mouth one of her favorite songs. White butterflies streamed out, landing on the glass. Then out came rays of gold dust particles and hidden fears. The mirror clouded, then cleared. The song fell back into her throat like water swirling down a drain. She walked out of her home and looked up at the clear white moon. She steadied herself, inhaled the darkness and from her lungs and chest she pushed a song out with all her might. Thousands of sparks flew into the air.

Bird Fall

"There's a bird loose in the house," I shout as my wife runs from the bedroom.

"I'm no bird," she shouts back.

"You're not a bird, I respond. "The bird is the bird."

"If I'm not the bird, then there is no bird," she says.

"Then what chased you from the bedroom? What is that rush of air that keeps blowing between us? that burp of chirps? that wild flinging?

"I don't see or hear anything, but you," she insists.

I point to the feathers at her feet, the white bird turds dolloped on the carpet.

"A few feathers and turds don't make a bird," she says. "If there were a bird in the house, we'd have to catch it to let it go."

"Now it's our bird, and it's ruining everything," I say.

"Ruining what? she answers.

A moment later, the bird slams into her cheek, and they both drop to the floor, dazed. "I told you there was a bird in the house," I say.

"I don't see anything," the bird answers.

Piece of Star

Late in the afternoon, I found a piece of star on the ground. I brushed it off and shook it until it glowed. The piece of star gave off a sweet scent, like a spice cake with loads of brown sugar. I tasted a little corner of it. It was soft and crumbly, not dusty or sharp. I liked the taste so I ate the rest of it in two bites. Craving more, I searched the grass and the ravine for the other pieces of star that must have fallen, but couldn't find any. Then I noticed the chickadees, finches, and phoebes carrying bits of star in their beaks, flying up into the trees, thousands of birds appearing at once. When I returned home, Greta kissed me on the lips. "Your lips are sweet," she said. "And you're glowing." I went to the bathroom to look in the mirror and didn't need to turn on the lights to see myself clearly, my face bright, my body emitting a blue and orange glow through my t-shirt and jeans. "I ate a piece of star," I admitted. "Do I need to take something?" Greta shook her head. "I'm sure it'll be out of your system soon enough." Later in the evening, I gave off so much heat and light that Greta stripped off all her clothes and jumped on top of me, laughing as if something new had come into her life—wanting to make love again. When we finished, she seemed happy, but then she couldn't sleep because the light was too bright. She piled blankets and comforters on top of me and put on a sleeping mask. By morning, my glow was gone.

Dirty Angel

"I'm your angel," he said. His face and body covered with dust, he stood in my doorway and handed me a leaflet. The ink was smeared, and the writing illegible. I crumpled it and gave it back, stuffing it in his shirt pocket. "I'm here to help you," he said. "Do you have a photo ID and something that might prove you're an angel?" I asked. "Look at my wings," he responded and did a full turn. He had two frail leaflike structures attached to his shoulders, filthy with ash and soot. "I wouldn't call those wings, more like giant eyelashes or a mesh for catching bugs." He put his hand on my arm. "Let me enter, brother." Still, I wouldn't let him pass. "Why do I need an angel?" I asked. The angel laughed. "That should be obvious." I peered into his dark, almost opaque, eyes to see if I could see a soul. For an angel, his face and body were surprisingly solid. A pale light emanated from his dusty skin. "Do something to prove you're an angel," I said. "Pass through the wall or raise a chair off the floor with your mind or vanish into thin air." He shook his head. "So much misinformation," he said. "That's what ghosts do, not angels. Are you going to let me enter?" I could see he wasn't going away anytime soon, so I stepped aside and let him in.

Shape

"You've lost your shape," my lover says. As she cleans the surface of the coffee table, she clicks her tongue and shakes her head without even looking at me.

I rise from the couch. "How so?" I ask....

She steps back, taking me in with her eyes. "You're shapeless," she says. "No other way to say it."

"That's impossible. Everybody, everything has a shape. What am I, an egg? a crooked trapezoid? a square with fuzzy edges?"

"You're more like a dollop of whipped cream or a blob of jam or foam in latte, though not so tasty."

"Can we stick to geometry," I ask.

"This seems more about chaos," she says, folding her dust rag. "Look in the mirror."

I walk into the bathroom. She's right. I'm shapeless. I can't find my belly or face. "How am I even able to wear clothes," I ask.

"Loosely," she says.

What causes someone to lose his shape? I wonder. Too much self preoccupation? or too little? I should have eaten better and taken care of myself.

My lover puts her arm around me, and her arm appears to float in fog. "I'm sure there's an exercise you can do to regain shape or some words you can chant or a yoga pose that might be perfect for just this condition."

"Maybe there's a doctor who specializes in treating this," I reply.

She smiles. "And even if there isn't...."

But something is happening in the bathroom light. Out of my shapelessness, a new shape is emerging, even if it is still in flux, even if we can't quite see it.

45

Orgasms on Amazon Prime

We ordered two dozen pairs of orgasms from Amazon Prime, 20% percent off per dozen. A box arrived two days later. Inside the box, the orgasms were packaged in pretty blue tinted plastic tubes, each with a cap and a ribbon. The fine print said: *Open only when ready to use. Each container good for two orgasms. Recycle after use.* "What if I want multiple orgasms?" Nathalie asked. "I guess you'll have to use mine then or we'll have to open two tubes, but it would be better to conserve our orgasms for really special moments." Tall and lithe-limbed, with lovely breasts, Nathalie picked up a tube and held it to the light "I don't see anything inside the tube," she said. I took it from her and scrutinized it near the window with the morning sun coming in. I couldn't see anything either. "I'll call Amazon," I said. The customer-service person explained that the orgasms were colorless, odorless like gas until the bottle is opened and then it's like the 4th of July or a nightclub with techno music blasting and strobes flashing. "Wow," I responded. I couldn't wait to try, even though Nathalie was skeptical because she only listened to hip hop and soul. In bed, we locked bodies and began kissing each other passionately, then I removed the cap. Rolling on top of me, she held her position, her breasts hanging just out of reach of my lips. "Do you feel anything," I asked. "I think I feel a tingling." "More like an itch," she said. It was a little bit like holding up your hand to an air conditioner to see if it's blowing cold air. Five more minutes—nothing. I called Amazon again. "It's like a broth—the rep explained, "you have to shake it up real good so everything mixes." So I shook and shook it, until the tube trembled, and bubbles collided against its walls. The cork blew off and hit the ceiling with a tremendous force, foam running over the sides of the glass.

"What just happened?" Nathalie asked. "Maybe the orgasms orgasmed," I answered, "without us." As we lay in the bed, the air felt sticky and warm, and small bubbles floated above us until they popped.

Lover

When I get into bed, a woman in black spandex tights gets in with me and kisses me. Her lips are sweet with a cherry lip balm. "Who are you?" I ask. "Sofia, your lover," she replies. I consider that for a moment as I sit up against the pillow to put some distance between us. "I don't know anyone named Sofia," I say, "and it's been months since my last lover left me." "She no doubt left you," she says, "because you couldn't remember she was your lover." I start to think about my former lover; I remember her face well enough, but her name eludes my grasp. Why did she leave me? I wonder. The woman in bed with me now does look familiar, the long silky blond hair and blue eyes. "Can you prove you're my lover?" I ask. "Yes, you have a scar under your right rib from a surgery you had as a child and a tattoo of ouroboros on your chest." "Good guess," I say, "but you're bluffing." She lifts off my t-shirt, and I don't resist. Then she peels off her own shirt, and we're face to face, squeezing each other, breathing each other's breath. Her warm skin feels familiar as does the touch of her hand. "Maybe you are my former lover," I say. "Why would you come back to me?" "I wouldn't," she says.

Somebody's Got My Hair—

I said to my lover, who stood in front of the mirror in a long white t-shirt brushing out her thick black hair. The silver brush glinted. I touched my head again and again, nothing but craggy dome and small patches of stubble over my ears. I felt a little tired and weak without my hair. How could I go out into the street as a bald man? "When's the last time you had your hair?" she asked. "Try to remember where you were." I could imagine myself with thick wavy brown hair, but I couldn't picture myself in a particular place. She put the brush down and came back to the bed, pressing her palm against my forehead. "No fever, no hair—did you lose it somewhere?" "No, it's hair; it's goes with me everywhere." She removed her hand. "Is it possible that someone from the office stole it while you were napping?" She looked deeply into my eyes, probing for the truth. "I don't work in an office," I said; "I don't work at all." "Did you possibly sell it to someone?" I shook my head. She knew I would never sell my hair. Was she trying to help or ridicule me? She got up and began searching through my drawers and the closets. "No sign of your hair anywhere, not even a single strand." I rose from bed and got dressed. She kissed me on the top of my head. "I fell in love with a bald man, not a man who has brown wavy hair." I smiled and kissed her back, though I knew she was in love with someone else.

Cuckold

When I came home one evening, I found my lover's clothes strewn on the floor and heard moaning noises. I caught her in the act—in the living room. "You're cheating on me with a couch," I shouted.

She stopped her gyrations and sat up. "I was just relaxing," she said. I had a hard day." Then she turned her anger on me. "I can't live with a man who doesn't trust me," she burst out.

"I trust you," I said. "I just don't trust the couch."

"You only see the bad in things, never the good." Unrepentant, she sprang up and began dressing. "Stay away from my couch," she ordered.

The next day, I stayed home from work to take care of the situation. After she left, I paid some mover I found on a listserv to drop the couch at the dump. Once it was gone, I felt relief.

When my lover came home that night, I greeted her with a big smile and a kiss. "I forgive you," I said.

She didn't apologize or even look guilty. Pretty soon she headed to the living room, no doubt to lie on the couch. I expected outrage, but instead she stared into the empty space where the couch used to be, too stunned to talk or perhaps in a trance.

When she came out of it, she went to work rearranging the room, shifting the comfortable easy chairs into the place where the couch used to be, angled toward each other as if carrying on a conversation.

"That's better," she said. This was too easy.

She pushed the ottoman in front of one of the chairs and then curled up in its arms. "I think I like this better," she said. "That couch was worn out anyway."

"I really hope this'll work out," I said, as she closed her eyes and let out a long breathy sigh.

Vampire

"Stop biting me," I said—scratching a new welt on my neck. She must have bitten me again while I was napping on the couch. Past midnight, the shades and windows were finally open, letting in the moonlight. "I'm not biting you," she said. "Don't scratch—it just makes it worse." I looked at her face, beautiful but pale, and the enlarged pupils of her eyes. She licked her lips and puckered her nose, but the tips of her ears flushed slightly as they did when she bluffed at poker. "Rebecca," I insisted, "you're lying." "What's wrong with you?" she answered. "Don't you want eternal life?" She had bitten me so many times over the past few weeks I had a red ring around my neck. Apparently, I had plenty of blood. I had noticed some changes though: a new vigor and the desire to stay up all night watching shows on Netflix. "You just think you're a vampire," I said. She kissed me on the cheek and then opened her mouth, the way vampires do in movies when their fangs come out, only her fangs were just large pointy canine teeth. I think she expected me to be frightened or at least impressed. "That's still not proof you're a vampire." "Sweetie," she said, "there are some things about me you're going to have to accept." She leaned in as if to kiss me again, but this time she bit into my neck and began sucking. Then, her lips bloody, she offered me her neck. "I'm not a vampire," I said, but bit in anyway and couldn't stop drinking.

Living with a Monster

"I'm a monster," Wilhemina says, standing in the glare of the kitchen lights. She has claws that resemble small paring knives and wings that surround her like a luxuriant fur coat. She may be a monster, but she is very beautiful, her face hard like a mirror, her eyelashes long and lush, and her dark hair falling to her knees. "It is possible," I reply, "that everyone is a monster." She raises her claw and slashes the air. "Not everyone rips apart their lovers," she says. "Not everyone eats them." "I'm still here," I counter. "You haven't devoured me." She smiles and touches my cheek with her claw lovingly, though she draws a little blood. "It's only a small cut," I say. I wash my cheek with warm soapy water, blot it dry with a paper towel and then I press a cotton pad against the cut. "It's dangerous living with me," she says. "I'll take my chances," I answer. "You seem very sure of yourself," she says. "Perhaps you are a monster." She searches my face, considering this possibility. "But you don't look like one." She brushes past me to open the refrigerator door. Peering inside, she is not happy with what she sees. "What's for dinner," I ask. "You," she answers and shuts the refrigerator, her face radiantly pale, ravenous.

Dinner Magic

"Don't you dare," my wife said as I stood up. "We have houseguests." "Exactly," I answered. "Now's the time to do it." We faced each other while the guests kept eating, their heads lowered to their plates. On the table were bowls of soup, salad dishes, plates filled with roast beef, gravy, potatoes, broccoli, glasses of red wine, bread baskets, olive oil dipping dishes, and much more. As I gripped the tails of the table cloth with both hands, our dog leaped to attention. Yes, I had had a few glasses of wine, but I felt confident and sharp. When I pulled the tablecloth out and whipped it around my shoulders like a cape, my wife screamed at me, "Why do you ruin every dinner party?" Contrary to her expectations, the dishes, plates and bowls didn't crash to the floor, didn't drop on our guests' laps, but rose off the table a few feet, hovering above us. "How do you expect us to eat?" one guest asked. Another threw down his napkin. "This has gotten ugly," he said, while another guest reached up and took some salad with her hands. "The dressing is excellent," she noted. "Get the dinner back on the table now—" my wife ordered, "in one piece." Not so easy, I thought. That part of the trick required me to chant the magic words four times without pausing. And that's what I did, but the dinner fell all over us. I had probably reversed two of the words. Before we could do anything about it, our dog ran off with several hunks of roast beef. Graciously, our guests began picking up the dishes. No one complained, and one or two even nibbled the potatoes while helping out. "That's quite a trick," one guest stated. "Yes," my wife commented, "not everyone can dump a whole dinner on his dinner guests." As our guests left, my wife stood at the door hugging each of them and apologizing. After locking the door, she returned to the dining room. "If you really knew any magic, you could erase this evening with a few words and a snap of your fingers." I nodded, but didn't try anything else. A moment later, she poured white vinegar on the rug, blotting up the stains.

Careful Not to Break the Chair

I get up to leave, but something pulls me back down. I look behind me, but there is only the chair. "You'll be late," my wife says, "Get a move." I get up again to leave, and then I realize the chair is stuck to my backside, and I can't straighten up. "Honey," I say, "I'm stuck to my chair, or really the chair is stuck to me, not the other way around." "Just like you to make such a fine distinction." She walks over to inspect the situation. Then she presses down on the back of the chair. "See if you can lift yourself away." Slipping forward a few inches, I wiggle a bit and push down with my feet but the chair lifts with me until my wife lets go, and I fall on my face, the chair intact. With considerable effort, she sets me upright. "Did you crazy-glue yourself to the chair so you wouldn't have to leave?" I shake my head. "I've got to break the chair. That's the only answer." I stand up as straight as I can, and the wood begins to give. She yanks me back to sitting position. "That's an expensive chair," she says. "You're not breaking it." "I can't walk into work with a chair stuck to me." "Who'll even notice? Their heads are all buried in work," she replies. I consider that for a moment. She has a point. Rarely do my coworkers notice me or anyone else. "Besides," she says, "several of them also have chairs stuck to their asses." "I've never noticed," I say and rise very slowly, careful not to break the chair.

Spot

A man and a woman make love to have a baby. Instead the woman gives birth to a spot. "He's our firstborn," the man says and names the spot Adam. "Let's try again," the woman says, "I want a daughter, not a spot." But the man is adamant that they should raise their spot first and then think about having a daughter. He feeds the spot whatever it'll eat, and soon the spot begins eating everything. "Now he's eaten my blue dress," the woman says, "and my diamond necklace." The spot denies it. "He's turned blue and his insides glint and glitter," she claims. "You can't blame him," the father says, "He's growing so fast, and he's hungry." One day, the father has to go out. "Be good," he says to the spot and then shuts the door gently. The woman grabs her cleaning fluids and brushes and begins scrubbing the spot, which is now the size of the kitchen. She pours bleach on it and cleanser. Though the spot loses some of its luster, it won't disappear or go away. Exhausted, she throws her brushes into the metal pail. When the man returns, he hugs the woman and kisses the spot. He notices that the blue has faded and that the margins of the spot are not as clear. "What has she done to you?" he asks. The spot refuses to lay the blame on his mother. The father again demands to know what has happened, and the spot swallows him. Now the spot has a healthy glow. "Are we good," the spot asks. The woman nods, but still wants a daughter.

After Birth

My lover gives birth to herself. It's a difficult birth, but she's shiny, and tears of joy fill her eyes as she lies under the sheets, her long dark hair falling down over shoulders.

"We agreed on a baby," I say.

"I'm your baby, she answers, giggling. "Take what you can get." She reaches up to me with her arms, as if she wants me to cradle her.

"But we wanted so much more for each other," I reply. She wraps her arms around herself and rocks back and forth, singing a lullaby.

"What about the bassinet—you won't fit."

"Let's take it back and exchange it for a larger size," she answers.

"And all the mobiles over the crib in the baby's room."

"I love mobiles," she says. "I couldn't ask for a better room." She kicks the sheets off. "Whether you like it or not," she says, "you're a father. Act like one."

"The baby needs her mommy," I say. "A father is not enough."

"Mommy needs a break, she answers "and some new clothes."

Sleep Gear

Sleep should be easy, but we get into bed with our retainers, our head gear and CPAP breathing masks. "Turn off the light," you say. "I can't sleep." "The light is off," I answer through my snorkel. Though the room is pitch dark, you untangle a few wires and feel around until you find your black sleep mask. How do you fit that over the other gear, I wonder, without breaking the elastic? Now you seem content, breathing quietly into the plastic tube. But the darkness rocks back and forth and then it shakes. "You're kicking again," you say. "No," I answer. "Those aren't my legs kicking." But when I reach under the covers and put my hands on my legs, they're like frogs hopping onto rocks. Just when my legs fall into an uneasy rest, just when you appear to be dreaming, whimpering and crying, a river enters the window, spilling on the floor. "A river—" I shout. "Shh," you whisper. "There is no river, and you say that every night." But I don't remember ever saying that. I turn to sleep on my side but the CPAP mask pushes against my face, so I roll onto my back. "You're thinking too hard," she says. "It's causing a disturbance." "What kind of disturbance?" "Like the sound of a ball repeatedly bouncing off a wall, like the moon plunging into a pool." "That's loud," I say. "I'll think more quietly." Now the river floods over us, but you don't seem to notice. I press on the LCD lights in my goggles. We're face to face behind our plastic masks. Tiny fish float between us.

Something Missing

There's something missing, but we can't figure out what it is. When we search for it, in our rooms, the closets, the attic, the garbage cans, we come back empty-handed. "It would help to know what we're looking for," my wife says. My son agrees, but adds, "We won't know that until we find it." He's always been precocious. "Let's retrace our steps again and do a really thorough search this time," I say, so all three of us search every room, open each drawer, turn things inside out that need turning inside out. Still, what's missing is still missing. "We've run out of places to look," my wife says. "It's gone." My son agrees, but asks: "What if something else is missing and we just don't know it yet?" My wife shakes her head. "Let's stop now? We're doing just fine without what's missing." My son agrees, but says, "We've got so much—who cares if a little is missing?" However, as the days go by, we spend our time imagining what might be missing, and it is always so much more than what we have.

Coyotes

At night, the coyotes stole our small dog and left tufts of hair, dots of blood. They stole our black cat and left a red ribbon, some footprints near an open door. They stole the fish out of the aquarium, and a puddle spread across the floor, glistening. At night, they breathed into the windows while the moon turned a blind eye. They licked the walls. They slipped into our bedrooms like whispers or particles of dust, watching us sleep. They licked our faces, slunk into our dreams. At night they stole our baby, her cries vanishing, a blanket crumpled on the floor. We washed the blanket and hung it on a clothesline. We chanted some words to keep the coyotes away, but our incantations and magic spells had no power. They came back with gifts, small toys, a pacifier with spittle, the baby's breath in a bottle. One morning, our baby yipped in her crib.

Section 4

Father and Son Singing

"You don't sing much, do you, son?" my father asks, sitting in his chair in the living room. He sings broken phrases, disconnected words, syllables that could be mantras the way he bends and stretches them. He sings melodies full of coins and fountains of cash. He sings a son who embraces his absence with real love. Now sitting in my chair, I sing too: bridges falling into holes, ties dangling from branches, monogrammed handkerchiefs sailing like kites. I sing the belly of my father, hands that rip cardboard boxes in two, his stubbled cheeks and chin, pillowcases stuffed with bills. I sing glossy wingtips sparking on the pavement, suits made of dust, the melody in the covered mirrors. His song ends with a sigh, mine with a gurgle. Neither of us can carry a tune.

Here Comes Trouble

Our mother is celebrating her 90th birthday. Sitting at a table with a tray of dahlias, zinnias, and white spray roses, she doesn't recognize my older sister and receives her kiss cheerfully. My sister doesn't recognize our mother, which is why she kisses her in the first place. My older sister also doesn't recognize her younger sister, who resembles her enough to be a twin. They embrace like long-lost friends, without seeming to remember their lifelong quarrel. I watch for signs of anger in their faces, but they're still smiling and hugging. "Nice party," the older one says. "Beautiful speeches," the younger one adds. "I like what you said about Mom." "What did I say?" the older one asks. "I can't remember exactly, but it was good." I hug them both. "Good to see you two getting along," I say. They pull away quickly. "I'm your brother, don't you remember?" "Yes, we remember," they say. "And you haven't changed, unfortunately." Then they look at each other for a moment, and their good will vanishes. "Stay away from me," my younger sister says and returns to her table. "I didn't want you to come in the first place," my older sister shouts." When I approach my mother, she loses her smile, shaking her head. "Here comes trouble," she says.

Punching Bag

My father punches me for hours each day. I think he's trying to make a point about something, but he's forgotten what that point is. I don't mind my father hitting me. His blows carry little force—really more like taps than blows. I do get bored standing in the middle of the living room, receiving his punches with nothing to distract me. Once, I asked that he turn on the TV, but he said he couldn't concentrate with a show on. When an occasional fly touches down on my nose, I swipe at it without intending harm. Sometimes I block a few of his punches just to keep him on his toes. When he lands what would seem to be a good shot, I pretend to be jolted. He tries out his combinations and throws flurries of punches until he can barely hold up his arms.

"Should we take a break?" I ask. He looks relieved that I've been the one to ask. "Five minutes," he says and drinks a bottle of water and eats some cheese to replenish his strength. And then we're back at it. My father grimaces and grunts and puts so much effort into punching me that I feel sorry for him. If I could knock myself out, I would.

Father's Chair

One night, my father's chair growled and bared its teeth at him. He had been sitting in it for years, slapping its arms, bouncing up on the cushions, talking to it.

"Maybe you should give your chair a night off," my mother said. "Sit on the couch," my sister added, "it's even more comfortable."

"Nonsense, I'm not moving from my chair," my father said, just before the chair opened its wide mouth and began to swallow him, head first.

We grabbed his legs, trying to pull him out, but the chair was stronger than the three of us, and father disappeared. "What kind of chair would do such a thing?" I asked.

My mother shook her head. "We bought it at a yard sale when we first got married."

"Let's get rid of it," my sister said. "It's dangerous." My sister left the room for a moment and returned with a small can of lighter fluid, but my mother took it from her.

"We're not burning the chair," she stated.

"We can't sell it," my sister said. "What if it eats someone else? We might get sued."

"It has to go to the dump," I said. "Your father loved this chair," my mother said and hugged us tightly. "And it's all we have left of him."

The chair appeared calm, at peace. Mother wiped the tears from her eyes. We cordoned it off with yellow tape and let it be.

After a few months, we removed the tape, and now Mother often sits in the chair, knitting a scarf of sighs.

Family

A mother weeps for her daughter, who has suffered more than she can take; and the daughter weeps for her daughter not yet educated in pain; and the granddaughter weeps
for her doll, the hair ripped and shredded, the body broken into pieces, the pieces collected like mementos. A little boy cups dirt in his hands, weeping for his dog, whose ashes have been scattered in the yard. His sister weeps for the damaged wing inside her chest, barely lifting. And a husband weeps for his wife, who won't recover; and the wife weeps for her husband, who lives with a hole in his heart; and the hole swallows love and sorrow, weeping as it feeds itself.

Rain of Ghosts

Without a wind or any kind of warning, the sky darkened, and ghosts rained down from the clouds, beating against trees and houses, against windshields. We ran for shelter, but the ghost rain pounded down so hard, many fell on the pavement. Many just gave up and stood still as if they had come up against a wall. Drivers slammed their brakes, staring into the face of ghosts clinging to their windshields. Ghosts soaked our clothing, streamed down our cheeks. We stood in puddles of ghosts. "Who is responsible for this?" someone shouted. And one yelled back, "You are." And someone else burst out, "These are not my ghosts." "They are now," another answered. Another jumped up and down trying to stomp out the ghosts as if they were flames on the earth. From the rain, ghosts rose up among us, breathing in our faces. "Let's send them back to the grave," several shouted with their fists clenched. "You can kill us if you want, "the ghosts responded, "but that doesn't mean we'll die." The clamor fell into silence. "If they won't die," I said, "there's nothing we can do." The rain slowed, softening to a drizzle until it stopped altogether, but the ghosts didn't disappear. They followed us to our homes and ate at our tables, their hunger growing greater with each meal.

Not Everything Was in My Father's Will

My father left me a CD with nothing in it and a record of all his closed accounts. He left me a hole in which to deposit old birds, the bust of the uncle he hated, old newspaper clippings of ads for clothing lines he was selling, the transistor radio he pressed to his ear to hear the ballgames, tales of his early days tossing feed to the chickens and chasing after the cow that wandered off into the field, the words to songs he no longer remembered, but still tried to sing. He left me a bridge to Paris the size of a chipmunk and a deed to a parcel of land on Mars. He left me the lingering scent of the Wildroot Hair Oil he combed through his thin wavy hair every morning. He left me the shadows inside his closet, waiting for the venetian blinds to be opened at dawn. He left me three pairs of glossy black wingtips and the sound of their shuffling over the sidewalks. He left me a leather jacket that held the shape of his round belly pressed against its buttons. He left me an envelope of Kennedy half dollars, each a talisman against curses and bad luck. He left me the country of hope floating in his brown eyes, the broken tree of his Hungarian ancestors, his favorite cliché about the past, "That's ancient history"—and his hunger for heavy stews.

Father and Son

In the mirror I see my father's face, his expansive dome, fleshy cheeks and nose, and rough chin. "Surprise," he says, "I bet you didn't expect to see me." He flashes his clownish smile. "Why am I seeing your face instead of my own?" "I like to think of it as our face," he answers. "But your face doesn't fit my body." "Our body," he says. I lift my shirt only to see my father's round belly, his forest of unsightly hair, a colony of brown spots and cherry bubbles. "We're a package deal," he says, "now that we're the same age." Like him, I have pains in my feet from walking and shift from one foot to another. Like him, I'm up and down all night and sleep only a few hours at most, my eyes always red-rimmed. "What did I do to deserve this?" I ask. "Let's just say that you had it coming," he says. I brush my hair vigorously, though there's not much left to brush. "You picked up that habit from me. You should really use a comb." I shut off the light, thinking he'll disappear in the darkness. When I turn it back on, it's my face in the mirror again. But I keep checking, turning the light on and off. Before I leave the bathroom, I catch another glimpse of my father's face. In the kitchen, I complain to my wife: "My father has stolen my face. Now I look like him." Touching my face, she laughs. "You just noticed?"

Smoke

A filament of smoke enters the home of a married couple through an open window. "Shut the window," the husband commands. She cranks the handle and locks the window. "That should do it," the wife says, but smoke thickens into a cloud and begins billowing in through the door and cracks in the walls. "Do something," he orders. He grabs a sheet and nails it to the door, and she sprays silicone in the cracks, but the smoke keeps coming, puffing from the vents and the floorboards. Soon it is so thick that they can't find each other. They call out as if on two ships passing in the fog, as if on islands floating off into the ocean. He opens his lighter and waves the flame to signal her. "I'm waving my lighter," he shouts, but the smoke is too thick for her to see it. "Shut it," she shouts back. "Our house could blow up." Dropping down on all fours, he crawls on the floor where the smoke is thinner until he can see her shoes and pants legs. "This way, this way." Gripping hands, they grope toward the windows. He opens a window, and then she opens another window and a door and then he opens another window, but instead of fresh air, a wind blows more smoke into their house. "We have to leave," she says, "before it's too late." "We can't leave," he says. "It's our home." She stumbles out the door, waiting for him to follow, while he stumbles through the house, waiting for her to come back in. The smoke never lets up.

Tea with Honey

She recalled for him the stained curtains, the rippled bread board, the serrated breadknife with its crooked teeth, the cracks in the air, the moths rising from the old woman's chest. "But you weren't there," he said. He walked over to the couch and sat down. "You only remember what I told you." She shook her head. "I remember what I remember: She was dying. I boiled the water, held the cup to her lips while she sipped the tea with honey." He held up his palm to stop her. "Why are you remembering this now?" Ignoring his question, she went on: "Even with all the covers and the hot tea, she shivered. I spread two heavy blankets over her." "I don't remember any of it," he said. "And I don't remember you," he shouted. "Shh," she whispered. Then she boiled water, made tea with honey. Sitting next to him, she brought the cup to his lips. "Drink," she said, and he did.

Slipping Away

She began slipping away from me—first an eyelash, then a strand of hair, first a word or phrase, then a plethora of sentences left unsaid, first a thought, then an island floating in the eye. Her silhouette evaded me like a forgotten name. "What's wrong," I asked. "Nothing," she answered, but my fingertip lost the curves of her body and then her body lost its curves. There were drawers left open, and clothes folded neatly that I had not folded. The traces of her scent vanished from the sheets and pillows, from the chairs and couches, from the clothing that hung in the closet. The ghosts of orchids hung their heads from the frozen pots. I heard her walking toward me. As shadows emptied into shadows, she returned to fix her hair in her mirror or smooth her face with cream. "I'm still here," she said. "Can't you see?" But her breath faded from the mirror, and soon even that was gone.

Ash

When the son touched his father's arm, his father turned to ash. He kneeled over the mound on the floor. "Treat me with respect," the father said, "even though I am ash." The son cupped some of the ash in his hands and carried it to a vase. He did this again and again until most of his father was in the vase, though some still clung to the floorboards and some stuck to his fingertips. "Why did you become ash," the son asked. "Because I was ash," the father answered. "And you touched a memory of your father." The son rubbed the ash until it disintegrated, leaving a gray stain on his fingertips. "I remember your death," he said, but I don't recall a memory of you." "What do you remember," the father asked. The son answered, "Only your ash."

Mother in the River

Mother didn't disappear like other mothers; instead, she became a river. Every afternoon, my father brought her flowers and begged her to come home, but she didn't answer his pleas, and soon the flowers disappeared, either drowning or flowing south. My sister waded into the water, small fish grazing her bare ankles. She whispered things to the river she didn't want father or me to hear. Sometimes she laughed— her face radiant with light—as if mother had spoken to her. Sometimes she disappeared beneath the surface, basking in mother's warm breath, she said. Stepping over broken glass and crushed cans, I walked the river bank until I knelt on the rocks by the water. I picked up a stick and stirred the ashes and bits of bone so that they would mix with the current, but some came back to cling to the rocks. At dusk, mother shut the shades of her windows and closed the door.

After the Burning

We held each other as our bodies turned to smoke and rose above the burning leaves. Hawks plunged through us, carrying bits of us in their beaks. We settled on roofs, clung to nests and nets. We drifted and drifted like cirrus clouds, like long tongues licking the sky, like glittery trails. Below, mounds of ashes crumbled or blew away. When the rain fell, we vanished, nowhere and everywhere at once.

Lost Memory

My sister stole a memory of mine from my house and took it home, hidden in her coat. I couldn't remember the memory, but there was an empty space on the sideboard under the window. "Give me back the memory," I said, standing outside her door. "And I won't report you to the authorities." She let me in. "Don't be ridiculous," she said. "Why would I steal a memory of yours?" It didn't take me long to find the memory, a blue jar sitting on the glass stand between two chairs. When I picked it up, she looked puzzled. "This is my place," she said. "These are my things." "Not true," I replied and unscrewed the lid. Emptiness wafted out with its stinging scent. Now I remembered something I had wanted to forget. I screwed the lid back on quickly and set it down. "That's my memory," she said. "You shouldn't have opened it." "Then what do you remember?" I asked. "Nothing—it's gone because you let it out." And as I stood there, angry at my sister, the scent of the memory evaporated, and all I could remember was the jar, and now that belonged to her.

How I Came to Write "Lost Memory": A Craft Story

Several months ago, while on the telephone with my sister, she began recounting the tragedies that befell her in childhood. There was quite a list, but one stood out to me. She said that my other sister had picked up the piano and heaved it at her, knocking her across the living room of our very small apartment and injuring her arm. "That's why I didn't pursue a career as a classical pianist," she said. I didn't see how my other sister, who struggled to carry her stack of books to school, could heave a piano, but determination can move mountains.

I told my eldest sister that I didn't remember this incident, but I did remember how in our childhood she had mysteriously started bleeding from every pore in her body. "We had to store you in the bathtub so you would drain into the tub." I recounted for her how mother and I collected her blood in pitchers and then she would drink it back down while our other sister practiced on the out-of-tune piano with the broken legs. Fortunately, a doctor from Barnes Hospital came up with a miracle cure. He taped her like a mummy until she stopped bleeding. She didn't remember, even though it had gone on for three years.

I then told her about how I had double pneumonia in second grade and was out of school for seven-plus months, and our mother was worried that the teacher would get the idea that I was just at home doing nothing but reading comics and watching TV, so she invited everyone over to the house and baked desserts and insisted that I recite the names of all the presidents. As I recited their names, the other students slipped out one by one, so by the time I got to Truman, I was talking only to my teacher, who applauded politely. When I got to the kitchen, they had polished off all the baked goods and vanished. When I came back to school, they had a new joke: "Friedman's room is so small he sleeps standing up." My sister said that she didn't remember that I had double pneumonia, not even the contraption with the hoses and the suction cups on the faucet in the bathroom.

Several weeks later, my sister began remembering bad things that happened to her in the past. "When I was in second grade," she said, "I had double pneumonia. I missed almost all of my elementary school years." Then she told me that Mother had baked for the kids in her class, and she had performed "Malaguena." "Wait a minute," I said, "You didn't have double pneumonia; I had it." We argued for a good hour about who had double pneumonia. "I had it too," she said. Then I remembered we didn't actually have a piano. She remembered that I wasn't her brother. I remembered that neither of us had another sister. "No more calls," we both shouted at the same time. Thus I lost a sister, but gained a new story, "Lost Memory."

Acknowledgments

My thanks to the editors of the following publications in which these poems first appeared:

Alcatraz: "Spring in Air" and "Flood"

American Journal of Poetry: "Beggar," "Spot," "Truth," "What's Left," "The Last Truth, and "Bad Day for the Shooters"

Body: "Voice in the Bush"

Café Irreal: "Dinner Magic," and "Dirty Angel"

Fiction International: "Coyotes"

Flash Boulevard: "Shape," "Cuckold," "Living with a Monster," "My Sister's Gift," "Light at the End of the Tunnel," "Family," and "Slipping Away"

Hole in the Head Review: "Tea with Honey," "Vacancies in the Cabinet," and "Night in the Prison"

Journal of Compressed Creative Arts: "Bird Fall" and "Hole in My Head" (Reprint)

MacQueen's Quinterly: Ram in the Thicket" and "Father and Son"

New Flash Fiction Review: "Vampire," "Mother in the River," and "Father and Son Singing"

New World Writing: "Hole in My Head," "Bombs," "The Singer Who Lost Her Voice," "Not Everything Was in My Father's Will," and "Lost Memory."

101 Jewish Poets of the Millennium: "Dream of the Garden"

Phantom Drift: "Piece of Star"

Plume: "Dead Animals" and "The Touch"

Poetry International: "Sleep Gear"

Serving House Journal: "Hole"

Solstice Anthology: "My Enemy" and "After the Burning"

Survision: "Catching the Monster," "Arrest," "Boy with Holes," and "Brotherly Love"

Unbroken: "The Ashes"

"Catching the Monster" appeared in *Prose Poem: An Introduction*, published by Princeton University. "Not Everything Was in My Father's Will" and "Lost Memory" were selected for the anthology, *Best Microfiction 2021*. "How I Came to Write Lost Memory: A Craft Story" was also published in *Best Microfiction 2021*, but under a different title. " "Tea with Honey," "Vacancies in the Cabinet," and "Night in Prison" were also published in the anthology *Dreaming Awake: New Contemporary Prose Poetry from the United States, Australia and the United Kingdom*.

My thanks to Nin Andrews for reading my initial manuscript and helping to select the poems that would become *Ashes in Paradise*. Thanks to Meg Pokrass, my writing collaborator, for reading the book at a much later stage and for her generous praise. Thanks to Dzvinia Orlowsky for her attention to my work over the last two decades and for her perceptive comments on this book. Thanks to Roy Nathanson for listening to so many of these pieces on the phone and for reading different versions.

Thanks to Celia Bland for her careful reading of my poems, her incisive criticism on this book and earlier books of mine. Thanks to Charna Meyers for her long-term friendship and for listening to my poems for the last thirty plus years. Thanks to William Doreski for all our meetings at Burdick's chocolate shop and for his comments on individual pieces in this collection and so many others. Thanks also to my friend poet Stevie Schreiner for his comments on individual pieces. Thanks to Ross Gay for his support and encouragement and for putting me in at least two of his "Delights." And my love and gratitude to Colleen Randall, who has lovingly lived with me and all my obsessive questions and the twists and turns of my poems, prose poems, micros and tales.

About the Author

JEFF FRIEDMAN is the author of ten collections of poetry and prose, including *The Marksman* (Carnegie Mellon University Press, 2020), and *Floating Tales* (Plume Editions/Madhat Press, 2017. His poems, mini-stories and translations have appeared in *American Poetry Review, Poetry, The New Republic, Dreaming Awake: New Contemporary Prose Poetry from the United States, Australia and the United Kingdom*, and *Best Microfiction 2021, 2022* and *2023*.

Cowritten by Meg Pokrass and Friedman, *House of Grana Padano*, a collection of fabulist microfiction, was published by Pelekinesis Press in 2022, He has also cotranslated and published two books of translations, *Memorials* (with Dzvinia Orlowsky) and *Two Gardens* (with Nati Zohar). He has received an NEA Literature Translation Fellowship, two individual artist grants from the New Hampshire Arts Council, and numerous other awards.

Friedman is married to the painter Colleen Randall, and they live with their dog Ruby, a mini Aussie, in West Lebanon, New Hampshire. He can often be seen in a large Wallaroo wide-brimmed hat and sunglasses walking 7–10 miles every day with Ruby, whose wondrous barking has become renowned all over New Hampshire and across the border in Vermont.

www.ingramcontent.com/pod-product-compliance
Lightning Source LLC
Chambersburg PA
CBHW021344090426
42742CB00008B/744